MW01245313

MEETING
THE
SWEET
GRASS

JOE GLUECKERT

ISBN 979-8-88751-351-5 (paperback)
ISBN 979-8-88832-155-3 (hardcover)
ISBN 979-8-88751-352-2 (digital)

Copyright © 2023 by Joe Glueckert

All rights reserved. No part of this publication may be reproduced, distributed, or transmitted in any form or by any means, including photocopying, recording, or other electronic or mechanical methods without the prior written permission of the publisher. For permission requests, solicit the publisher via the address below.

Christian Faith Publishing
832 Park Avenue
Meadville, PA 16335
www.christianfaithpublishing.com

Printed in the United States of America

CONTENTS

ACKNOWLEDGMENTS

Special thanks go out to my neighbor, friend, and proofreader Eda de Ruiter-Dotzek, for her diligence and inspiration throughout this book. She was an instrumental grammarian throughout each of these stories.

INTRODUCTION

This book is a collection of short stories set in Montana in the last years of the 1960s. They tell the tale of a young stranger becoming a summer season hired hand on a fourth-generation family ranch. Here, the Old West traditions mix with the hard work of a devout family saving their home in more modern times. Here, you will find a bear hunt, good endings to bad mistakes, close encounters with wild cows, cowboys being tossed through the air from a bucking bronco's back, or meetings with scary people with even scarier propositions. You even find some lessons from the Word of God about wise farming and the importance of rest for the land, and Sundays for people. These memories are suitable for ages seven to ninety-nine and for all who enjoy cowboy life and adventures.

Meeting the Sweet Grass is as traditional as Montana itself, with its typical characters, rodeos and cowboys, shepherds, and Native Indians. It's a glimpse of *The Big Sky Country*, as seen through the eyes of a wide-eyed high schooler, who is a quarterback in fall, a cowboy/rancher in summer, and there inhaling the scent of the sweetest grass and learning real-life lessons.

SWEET GRASS 1

Before the Sweet Grass

In 1967, my father was a jack-of-all-trades, but he was primarily a carpet and linoleum installer. His business took him all over the central-southern parts of Montana, from Bozeman to Billings and from Harlowton to White Sulphur Springs. His territory included Yellowstone National Park and Cook City. For as long as I can remember, I was taken out of school to help my dad with big jobs or on jobs over a hundred miles away that he wanted to complete in one day. Many customers had commented how well we worked together without much talking, and the jobs smoothly flowed into the completion of more modern floors.

The old green-and-white International panel truck could fly down the highway. I don't think Dad ever drove under eighty miles per hour, and with all the windows down and the wind whistling through, most conversations were limited to one or two words because it was impossible to hear each other. That only changed during the winter because you'd freeze with the windows down. The old heater did not work too well either even though it took up most of the floor space in the passenger seat.

On those long, cold drives, I usually lost myself in imagining I was a mountain man like Jim Bridger or a cowboy on a long trail drive from Texas to Montana. I often traveled back in history, ignoring the fence lines and everything but the natural shapes and mountains we followed along the rivers rushing downstream. I loved the mountains from the Beartooth to the Bridgers to the Crazy Mountains. And I often thought the shell cliffs that ran for miles were buffalo jumps more so than they probably were.

Dad often said that he was going to pay me, but he never did that I can remember in spite of the many compliments on our work from our customers. But around Christmas, he tried to make up for it. I remember especially the winter of 1967 when I got a motorcycle for Christmas. Dad teared up like a little kid, and I cannot explain how excited I was. After the shock of the motorcycle came an even bigger present when he told me that I was going to have a job on a ranch next summer at a little place called Melville somewhere between Big Timber and Harlowton. This was as good as winning the State Football Championship in my mind.

Suddenly, all the promises that were never realized did not matter anymore, and the discussions about a partnership with Dad in the carpet business flew out the window. It seemed like the world was smiling at me. I also was the freshman starting quarterback in 1967 with even talk of next year making varsity for sure. All of it together seemed like a dream come true. My best friend Dave said, "All the cylinders are firing in your favor." He couldn't believe how excited I was about going to the middle of nowhere for a summer job on a ranch at the foot of the Crazy Mountains.

In the month of May, I turned sixteen; and a few weeks later, I had my driver's license, both of which were needed to work on the ranch. Work with my dad was slow through the winter and spring, and when June came, my suitcase was already packed, and the anticipation of being on a ranch all summer made it hard to sleep. Dad and I had a carpet-laying job in Big Timber, and the grandmother from the ranch was picking me up there around 4:00 p.m., so I hustled a bit more to make sure there was no holdup on my side. Dad made the unusual move of stopping for a hamburger lunch and told me all about his experiences as a kid working on a ranch north of Bozeman. My excitement kept increasing as the day wore on, and I felt the kind of frustration you feel when a tire just won't fill up with air.

SWEET GRASS 2

Meeting Grandma

We had just folded our arms to wait for Grandma when a dusty car pulled up with Grandma's smiling face behind the wheel. I noticed the only part of the car that didn't have dust on it was what the window wipers had cleaned. Since I have allergies, I wondered if I should have brought extra allergy medicine with me, which for me in those days was cough syrup.

Grandma remembered Dad, who introduced me with the embarrassing, "And this is Joey."

Grandma shook my hand and said, "Pleased to meet you, Jody."

After another very long exchange, I definitely had the feeling that Grandma did not have a lot of time to make visits. So I pulled out my suitcase and cowboy hat and set them by the trunk of the dust-ridden Ford.

After a few more formalities, Dad said, "You'll love these people, Joe," and we went to our separate vehicles and drove off, following each other until we hit the highway.

The first thing I noticed in Grandma's car was that should we get in a wreck, we would be killed instantly by debris flying from the dash. I wasn't sure if Grandma was looking through the steering wheel to protect herself from that happening or because of the way the sun was hitting the windshield. Another thing that struck me right away was that suddenly, Montana seemed to have a speed limit, and Grandma would not speed. I can't remember ever being passed by so many assorted vehicles.

Our conversation wandered from high school to allergies, which was a major highlight because she also had allergies. We scratched the surface of history and moved on to religion, and we exchanged our Catholic and Lutheran points of view, Grandma then recited a Bible verse, "The righteous will live by faith." This truth out of the Book of Romans in the Bible became the dominant subject, and I enjoyed Grandma's understanding of them and that my Catholic faith didn't seem to be foreign to her at all.

We passed Melville's few buildings, turned off the Harlowton highway and headed toward the majestic snow-covered Crazies. The little Melville Lutheran Church sat out in the middle of a picturesque hayfield with its white lap siding, making it stand out among the tall green hay and those purple Crazies rising up behind.

Grandma explained, "This is Norwegian country. They settled here because it reminded them of home." She said that we had about twenty minutes to go. My nerves started to get the best of me, and I asked if they had electricity.

She laughed. "Oh, yes, and we even have running water in the nearby creek."

My look made her laugh some more with a little sarcastic tone as if she was making fun of me. But she assured me with an apologetic pat on my knee, "We have everything your town has except paved streets and sidewalks."

I thought she had probably never met such a city slicker as me before.

Soon, we dropped off a plateau-like area into a creek bottom and turned off the gravel county road onto a private dirt road. *Will we be here for a while, and will this be home?* A white two-story house stood out with its green roof and a chain-link fence separated its plush green lawn from the rest of the barnyard. Geese and chickens hurried out of the way, and a few milk cows ignored us as we passed them. Several horses bucked away like they were saying, "Don't even think about getting near us."

We pulled up, and a man and a woman stepped out of the side door just before Grandma came to a stop. I was introduced by Grandma, "And this is Jody, everybody."

Vicky, a tall barrel-chested man stepped up and said, "Well Jody, we are glad you came."

While shaking my hand, he nodded at his wife, Maxie, who said with a Dale Evans smile, "Nice to meet you, Jody." Next came Victor, Vicky's dad, to shake my hand and welcome the new hired hand, and Maxie said, "We're about to have dinner, so go in and wash up."

SWEET GRASS 3

Getting to Know You

Stepping through the side door, the view opened up to a big kitchen and a huge table. My eye caught the old wood-burning stove next to the propane stove. I thanked God that, yes, there was electricity, and the kitchen was bright and cheery. There had to be at least a dozen chairs around the huge rectangular table. Without a tablecloth, the wood surface and its stain-marred finish displayed its age and that through the years, many had sat around it.

While I waited by the outer wall lined with windows, I immediately noticed the many large platters of food, especially the one in the middle with steaks piled high on it. Just then, there was the sound of another door opening and stamping feet with the sound of water running and some groans coming from an open doorway that led to the back of the kitchen. After a little small talk, everyone sat patiently waiting for whoever was making all the noise in the mudroom.

Finally, Vicky announced, "This is our son, Duane, and this is Jody, our summer help this year." Duane was definitely a cowboy, with slicked back wet hair and a belt with a big silver buckle with Lazy T, X engraved on it around his waist. With a big mischievous grin, he scooted around the table and sat right next to me. Then everyone bowed their heads, and Vicky's boisterous voice thanked the Lord Jesus for this meal.

Mashed potatoes and gravy and the meat platter were soon passed around the table, and Maxie said, "Jody, if you need anything, please don't be shy!"

Grandma chuckled, "You might have to go to our little creek to get it!" Then she cheerfully began telling everyone that I thought we did not have electricity or running water, and everyone laughed, throwing in a couple of dirty digs here and there. I took it that they were letting me know I was in the family now because most of the sarcastic digs were followed up with laughter, and Vicky's sense of humor immediately made you feel like you were okay in his book.

Duane was about a year older than me, but he seemed far more mature. He laughed quietly, trying not to, with every bite. Grandpa asked about a field by name, and the talk got serious. Duane gave his assessment of the grasses by name also and reported that the yearlings looked to be at a good weight already. He then complained about one of the cow dogs not paying attention, and Vicky said, "Yeah, Cindy is a little dingy at times."

I got the impression that animals and grasses were the number one subject around this table. Grandma started complaining about "all those women," and everyone laughed, and I took it that she belonged to some women's club. Then she had another complaint about "Dorothy's egg count going down."

Duane asked me, "Did you bring your football?"

"Yeah, I did."

"Well, we will have to see about that big gun of yours."

Maxie interrupted, "Dessert is coming, and then we'll show you your room."

Vicky added, "Yeah, it's the bunkhouse!"

And Grandma giggled, "Out down by our running water, Jody!"

I guess my expression gave everyone a reason to laugh, and Grandpa offered, "At least you'll be able to get away from this hen pecking."

Apple pie was dessert and whipped cream in a huge bowl. *Wow*, I thought, *I must have died and gone to heaven.* I was hoping to gain some weight for the next football season, and boy, I believed I had come to the right place.

After dinner, I got my suitcase out of Grandma's trunk, and Vicky and Duane led me to the bunkhouse. It looked like a dollhouse, really, neatly painted white with a little front porch and little girly curtains tied in the windows. Inside it had a kitchenette and front room, and in the back were the bathroom and bedroom. Vicky apologized for the girly accommodations but explained this was their daughter's place before she got married about a year ago.

Duane smiled. "Dad tells all the hired hands that story!"

They both started laughing, and I realized I must have had a very gullible expression on my face the whole time. Before that thought had run its course, Vicky added, "Don't worry, Grandma took all the girl clothes out of here, so help yourself to the closet and the dresser drawers. It's all yours, and Grandma will be your maid, so don't worry about the decor. She won't let you change it! You can come to the front room and watch TV if you'd like, or you can hang out here or look around the place. Make yourself at home."

They left, and I sat on the bed, thinking that now I would not be able to tell my friends how rough the bunkhouse was. I found the front room, and after thanking Maxie for the nice dinner, I found a seat close to her, and she said, "You're welcome. We're looking forward to your help and company too."

The front room was bigger than the kitchen and had four huge leather couches lining the walls. There was a small TV set, and everyone's eyes were focused on it. I don't remember the program, but it was a comedy in its day. Vicky finally stood up with a stretch and a big yawn, "Well, Jody, you and I have an early date tomorrow with the leafy spurge, so I'll be getting you up early."

I took the hint, said my good nights, and headed to bed in the dollhouse. Wow! That one took some getting used to!

SWEET GRASS 4

A Day in the Life of a Ranch Hand

The dollhouse door opened between 4:00 and 4:30 a.m. with Vicky's booming voice, "Jody, it's morning, nearly daylight in the swamp! Are you a ready teddy?" His infectious laugh started answering his own question.

I yelled at the silhouette in the open door, "Yes, I'm up, I think."

"Okay! Meet me by that scrap iron pile behind the welding shed!"

Stumbling around getting dressed and making my way out of the dollhouse, the smell of fresh manure hit me right away and almost made me want to plug my nose. Making my way to the back gate near the mudroom, I saw Vicky already up on the one-thousand-gallon tank trailer, with a huge fire hose hoisted up there with him. The old gray-and-red Ford tractor and the pump were running, and Vicky yelled down, "Good morning, Jody! It's a nice morning for spraying, no wind! Hey, turn off that valve behind you!"

I turned and found what looked like an antique cast-iron handle above the old fire hose. Then before I got it completely turned off, I heard a huge splash of water hitting the ground on the other side of the tank. Vicky threw the hose down, and the water made a big mud puddle. With that, it quieted down because the water pump automatically shuts off. I handed him a huge box of laundry soap, and he emptied all of it into the water tank trailer. Next, I gave him the concentrated weed killer in a two-gallon jug. With that, he called down, "What do you think, two or three gurgles?"

I didn't know, so I held up three fingers while shrugging my shoulders.

Vicky laughed. "Okay, four then!"

I noticed Vicky had knee-high rubber boots on, which took me by surprise. He climbed up on the tractor and waved me aboard. In half a yell, "Have you driven a tractor before?"

"No!"

"Well, here's the gearshift, and here's the throttle, and the clutch and the brakes are down here. I'll go slow, and you'll catch on."

We pulled out toward the way Grandma had come in yesterday, and we got about seventy yards past the house when he stopped the tractor and said, "Okay, you're driving now, Jody."

I wasn't sure if this lesson had lasted even five minutes. I climbed in the driver's seat, and Vicky sat on the rear wheel's fender.

Then he said, "I have one more thing to add. Don't throw me off this tractor, or you might not get paid for today!"

Wow! That made me just a little nervous, so I started as slow and smooth as possible. We hit the main road, and Vicky said, "Make a left, and you can open her up a little."

After my left turn, I pulled the throttle to open her up a little, and Vicky shouted, "It might help if we were in a bit higher gear!"

We both laughed with me half yelling, "Sorry!"

As we climbed out of the creek bottom, Vicky said, "You need to listen to the tractor and the trailer altogether. If something doesn't sound right, stop and check it out, okay?"

I yelled, "Okay!"

"Now might be a good time to stop, Jody!"

Holy cow! I thought, *What the heck?* I stopped in the lane. "What's wrong, Vicky?"

"I have to pee is all."

And I thought to myself, *I hope he doesn't expect me to listen for that too.*

Vicky climbed back on and laughed a little. "You're doing fine. We'll be going in the next gate off to the right."

10

The sun was nearly peeking over the eastern butte. These plains looked like rolling hills that seemed to stretch out forever in front of us. We turned in, and Vicky hopped off and said, "Let's see how tough you are this morning. But before you come here showing off, make sure the tractor is in neutral and pull the brake on."

I saw the gate had four poles and barbed wire strung across the opening. "Okay, I'll let you open it, Jody!"

I pushed the poles together where the two wire loops held the gate closed, and nothing was happening, except my face was getting red from holding my breath and trying to squeeze the two poles together to release the top loop of wire. "Okay, Jody, I'm going to show you an old cowboy trick, and don't spread it around. Lean into the pole with your shoulder and, with your other hand, lift off the loop. Like I said, don't spread this trick around!" He laughed and drove the tractor through the gate. "Yeah, Jody, leave the gate open." Then he stopped, pulled out this long red garden hose with a brass nozzle and trigger, and pointed, saying, "Just follow me along the fence line now."

We slowly started spraying a weed called leafy spurge, which to me looked like yellow mustard. The slow-moving job gave me lots of time to scan the countryside. To the north, it stretched forever; and to the east, west, and south, the mountains seemed to horseshoe us in. It felt and looked like the Wild West. We sprayed for nearly four hours. Now and then, Vicky would point at a rabbit or a bunch of pheasants suddenly taking off in front of him.

Finally, he stopped, turned around, and rolled the hose up to start back to the home place. I rode back on the fender and shut the gate with no problem. We rolled into the barnyard and saw the four cow dogs holding fourteen cows against the milking shed. Vicky stopped the tractor and turned it off, and I followed him to the shed. He stopped and turned. "Why don't you stay here until I get the shed open?"

I watched him walk through the milk cows who stepped aside. The shed door rolled open, and the dogs nipped at the cows' heels to chase them in. Vicky waved. "Come in, Jody, and close the door behind you."

At that same moment, both nostrils were blasted with the stench of fresh manure. I made a face, and my eyes started watering.

Vicky laughed. "So you don't like the smell of my gold?"

"Gold?" I said, "Man, this is horrible!"

Vicky smiled. "Without this smell, we wouldn't have a ranch. Let's get you started milking old Sally here. She has only three tits, and she's a gentle gal if you're gentle with her. You have to squeeze your fingers one at a time top to bottom and a little pull will help."

I started milking, the shed door opened, and Grandma and Grandpa entered with buckets and little T-board stools. After Duane showed up, all the cows were milked in no time. We men carried the eight three-gallon buckets to the spring house where the milk separator was, and Duane and I finished the chore of putting the cream in a big can and all the skim milk in a bucket for the pig trough.

You quickly find out why pigs are called pigs. They have atrocious eating habits. Duane had to stop one pig from climbing into the feeding trough as they fought and squealed to get into the best position. We washed the buckets in the spring house and then were off through the mudroom for a breakfast of pancakes with whipped cream and syrup. Vicky said grace, and we dug in.

Water and irrigation were the main subjects, with Vicky revealing with a smile how much I liked the aroma of the milking shed, and Grandma adding, "Don't you bring that aroma into your bunkhouse, Jody, or we'll be cleaning the milking shed out for your new bunkhouse."

That definitely wasn't a picture I looked forward to.

SWEET GRASS 5

About Water, Gophers, Sparks, and a Tub

At breakfast, I learned about "water rights" being established at the turn of the century. The "V" dot ranch had established its "water rights" in the 1880s. The ranch's water gate was above the Anchor Ranch close to the western Crazy Mountains.

After a lot of talk about water and irrigating, Vicky, Duane, and I climbed into the old Jeep Wagoneer pickup, and one of the dogs jumped into the bed of the truck. We followed the same path we had earlier this morning, and our conversation centered on shooting and hunting. I learned Grease was their hunting dog and would never miss a ride in this old Jeep.

Once we reached the lane, Vicky stopped the Jeep, and both doors opened simultaneously, so I thought it was a potty stop again, but no, they pulled out the .22 rifles, loaded them, and started looking for gophers on a hill to the south. Both Duane and Vicky had a whistle that made a running gopher come to a complete stop in its tracks, rise up, and look around. The little guy was soon shot, and this was their target practice time to and from the hayfields morning, noon, and night. They got me shooting and had some good laughs at my horrible performance. Vicky told me with that cowboy smirk of his, "Jody, we're not going to let you shoot here if you keep missing the hill because Grandma will be mad at you if you break a window in the bunkhouse!"

Duane said with his quiet grin, "So far, Jody, you're doing good because we see nothing but dust out there."

Vicky added, "You know, this is a rare rodent control pesticide. It doesn't work unless you hit the gophers."

After emptying the guns on the scattering gophers, we continued down the lane, turned onto a rough road, and soon reached several manicured and cultivated fields.

We stopped in the middle of a huge pasture, which held the ranch's cattle, about two hundred head. Our mission was uphill from these pastures where we grabbed a couple of shovels and put on hip waders, and Vicky handed me an eight-foot-long pole rolled in canvas.

About a hundred yards away to the east, there was an irrigation ditch cut along the base of the butte. Vicky explained that on the other side of it was the winter wheat and south of it, the barley. Duane stabbed his shovel into the bank of the ditch and started walking north along it. Vicky and I rolled out the canvas around the pole, which looked like the wooden fence post at the lower gate by the lane. We made a dam securing it with dirt, and in the distance, Duane raised another temporary dam just like ours.

Before he made it back to us, water flowed up into our canvas dam and started spilling over the banks of the ditch onto the hayfield below. Vicky said, "It's all about gravity and elevation. God made it work to run downhill!" We opened a few more places along the ditch's bank to get the water to flood and spread more over the hayfield. Vicky yelled out after half an hour or so, "Jody, you're a natural irrigator. You look like you can make water flow uphill!"

Grease, a Chesapeake Bay Retriever, liked to hang with Vicky. He'd spit on his glove and throw it, and Grease would fetch it. Vicky and Duane were talking about checking on the "big field" and a new bull, so we climbed back into the Jeep, and I sat in the back of the bed to dry my jeans a bit in the sun. We rocked and rolled slowly along the hayfields, and I got to open another gate with the old cowboy trick using my shoulder and close it after the Jeep rolled through. When we reached the "big field," we made a circle and found the bull they were looking for surrounded by about thirty cows who seemed to like him. We headed back to the lane, made a short stop at the shooting gallery, and headed home for lunch.

Lunch was a full-course meal like every other one. There were no sandwiches to speak of but always bread to push stragglers like peas onto your fork. After lunch, I learned what the four couches in the front room were for. We all grabbed one, stretched out, and closed our eyes for from fifteen minutes to sometimes an hour. After a nap, Vicky and I headed out to change the irrigation set again and then met Duane in the shop. He had arranged some old railroad tracks on the concrete floor of the shop to make a cattle guard between their access road and the county one.

Vicky moved and measured, and then we headed down to measure the intersection where an old culvert lay below their road, parallel to the county road. They decided on a six-foot span and back at the shop started welding. Sparks covered the concrete floor, and the static charging sound of raw electricity barked out at every touch of the welding rods. They gave me the task to smooth out some of the rough welds.

Later that afternoon, Duane and I made another irrigation set change. When we got back Grandma, Grandpa and Vicky were milking already. When we came into the milking shed, Vicky said, "Old Sal is patiently waiting for you, Jody!"

Grandpa added, "I think you are her new favorite!"

Then it was dinnertime, and afterward, I did a little more snooping around. I even hiked westward to what was called the Cooke City Highway, ran back, and had to ask about showering because the dollhouse bathroom only had a toilet and sink. Off the mudroom, there was a bathroom with a tub only, no shower! Wow! But it had hot and cold running water, and it really felt good to get cleaned up. I went right to bed afterward.

This became the daily routine at the ranch until haying season. The afternoon jobs changed from fencing to mowing the lawn, looking for strays once in a while, and also cowboy stuff like moving yearlings around from one pasture to the next to let the wild grass rest. I was what you call one tired pup for those first couple of weeks.

SWEET GRASS 6

About Girlfriends, Flashing Skies, and Snow in July

The daily routine became the norm with Vicky's wake-up calls every morning. Though they were different every day, they always came before sunup when we had to spray the dreaded leafy spurge. Several weeks had hurried by, and I noticed my cowboy hat started to look like it belonged in the mudroom with the rest of the other well-worn hats. I began wearing waders and was changing the irrigation sets by myself with Grease in the old Jeep pickup.

When you are flooding the ground, you discover you're disturbing a lot of wildlife, like snakes and gophers and, once in a while, a badger or porcupine trying to get out of the water's way. I had also borrowed an old .22 Browning rifle and made my regular stops on the lane to and from the hayfields to help lower the gopher population. I could even whistle and make them stop in their tracks once in a while.

When you're irrigating by yourself and you pull the temporary canvas dam full of water, you have to get the next one ready to set up at the next spot, leapfrogging them down the ditch. I liked doing it running once in a while with the waders on, and Grease usually ran ahead. She certainly could clear the way in a playful romp. Grease was interested in just about everything we stirred up with the water flooding and blanketing the ground, and she would bring me most of her finds. She had a good understanding of skunks, porcupines, and badgers.

One day, we cornered a little mink, and I caught it and threw it in the cab of the Jeep. Boy, that was a big mistake! It stank to high heaven for at least a week. Vicky and Duane gave me a bad time about letting Grease ride in the cab with me. She usually sat right next to me, and Duane often told me, "You know, Jody, your girl-friend is pretty darn ugly!" Grease even started accompanying me on my walks or after-dinner runs, and even the cow dogs ran along from time to time. Vicky would say sarcastically, "What are you doing with my dogs?"

Later that summer, there were a series of lightning storms so bad and close you could smell the sulfur in the air. On one particular night, while we were watching Johnny Cash, sparks suddenly shot out of the on-and-off switch of the TV just as the dark sky lit up for a long second. The TV screen went black, and Vicky calmly got up, hit the off button, and said, "Well, I guess it's bedtime, Jody," with his big grin and a half a laugh following.

That night, all the dogs were waiting for me at the door of the dollhouse, and I let them all in. Ticky, an old black Australian Shepherd, needed help, so I lifted her up on the bed. The next morn-ing, I heard Vicky's boisterous wake-up call, "Jody! What are you doing to my dogs!" Then he continued in a good-natured tone, "I hope you cleared this with Grandma!"

So we all scrambled out of the dollhouse, and Grease and I were off to the old Ford tractor with the water tank to start spraying again.

One evening, Vicky and Duane were shooting at an old burn barrel with Duane's new .45 pistol while I was stretching to get ready for my run. Vicky said he'd like to see Duane and me race. I said, "Sure, I would be game! When do you want to do it?"

Duane smiled. "Right now!"

"Okay, I'll wait for you to change and meet you here."

Duane looked at me kind of funny. "I'm ready now. I don't need to change!"

"You're going to race me in your cowboy boots?"

"Yup!"

So we lined up on the dirt entrance road toward the county road, and we were going to race to the small granary about fifty yards away. I asked one more time, "You're sure you'll be okay?"

"Yup! I'm only running to the granary. You can run farther if you like."

Vicky said, "Are you boys racing, or are you just going to talk about it?"

We both half-mumbled, "Yup!"

"Okay! On three. One, two, three!"

And we took off in a flash! Duane beat me so bad it was embarrassing. I heard Vicky laughing back at the starting line, "Jody! This was a sprint, wasn't it?"

And Duane, rubbing it in too, "And these are my slow cowboy boots!"

It was a long embarrassing kidding session, lasting about a week. Vicky even gave me a pair of old worn-out cowboy boots with the remark, "These are for practicing, in case you are planning a rematch one of these days."

One night, Grease came barking at the dollhouse door. She stood up on her hind legs, scratching at the door's window. When I opened the door, I saw she was all excited and wanted me to follow her. I sensed this was going to be a hunt, so I ran to the Jeep to grab the old Browning, and we went running toward the little granary. Grease started pawing at the lower tin door, and with the Browning in my shoulder ready to shoot one-handed, I flung the granary door open, and all I saw was huge teeth coming at me, and Grease and I bolted, running for our lives!

Raccoons are vicious when cornered and have dangerous-looking teeth. When I told Vicky the story the next morning, he smiled and, with a cautious tone in his voice, said, "I'm glad you didn't shoot because I'd hate to see a hole in my granary. Worse yet, you could have hit Grease if that raccoon had run off between your legs!"

The closer haying season came, the harder we worked on mowers and rakes to get them all ready. The "farmhand" was a front loader attached to the tractor to scoop up the hay from the windrows, and Vicky's invention "the haystacker" were lubed and greased. We used hay wagons and had a corral where the hay was loosely stacked. Vicky preferred the loose haystacks because, with three men, we could hay faster than the places where they baled their hay.

One time during haying season, Vicky said in the afternoon, "Why don't you go in and start milking the cows."

Duane and Vicky were finishing up the last couple of hay wagons, so I milked nearly all the cows until Grandpa came and milked the old Guernsey. My forearms hurt for nearly a week. The following summers, there were never that many cows again, and I was thankful that I never had to milk thirteen cows by myself again.

On the Fourth of July, some of the families and ranch hands met at the Anchor Ranch for fireworks. It was a simple affair, but there was a lot of talk and plenty of watermelons, cakes, and pies. I don't remember any beer, but there was coffee and lemonade. During the whole drive up and back, I was teased about the Sergeant girls and warned I'd better not be sneaking off with them because Mr. Sergeant would be watching me the whole time.

Maxie came to my defense and said, "They don't even know Jody! And those girls are probably going to be busy hosting."

Vicky sarcastically added, "For Jody's sake, let's hope so!"

After a surprisingly spectacular fireworks show, driving home, I got the same treatment. Vicky asked me, "Did you even meet the Sergeant girls?"

"No, not unless they are Mrs. Sergeant's sisters-in-law."

Maxie elbowed Vicky. "You'd better not go there. Let's drop it!"

I think there was definitely an inside story somewhere, and that line of joking was dropped like a rock.

One Fourth of July, I was expecting to spend the day haying when Vicky opened the door and said, "Jody! We're going to the state fair today, so if you want to go, put on your city duds. We can't hay in the snow."

I took a quick look out the bedroom window and saw two inches of snow on the ground, so we went to Billings instead of haying, which was really nice. I learned Vicky and Duane were people watchers, and it was fun listening to them guessing what the different passersby did for a living. We had lots of fun, games, and food all day, but we had to leave earlier than anyone of us wanted to because we had a few cows to milk at home.

SWEET GRASS 7

Who Shot That 350-Plus-Pound Bear?

In the same summer that the sparks flew out of the TV, we took a ride up to what was known as the high country. This grazing pasture rose up quickly into a butte, leading to the timberline just below the Crazy Mountains. Vicky had decided to put his yearlings there for this particular summer. About a week after the series of horrible lightning storms, we drove up there in the Jeep. Before we got to the high country's gate, we saw what appeared to be dark rocks lying in a lower section of the butte.

As we got closer, we saw that what looked like rocks were a cluster of dead yearlings. We counted fourteen head struck by lightning. What really shook us up was that so many had been killed. The lightning had boiled their hooves, leaving just a permanent bubble behind. Three steers had been thrown over the nearby barbed wire fence. Their hides were torn open, and all the flesh was charred and burnt to a crisp. Maggots were already feasting on them, and it looked like a bear was enjoying the maggots for an appetizer.

It was immediately decided to move the yearlings out of the high-country pasture before something like this could happen again. Vicky said he had never seen anything this bad before. One or two yes, but never fourteen all at once. Even the knoll was charred black, and we assumed the fork of lightning must have danced there like it did the night when it blew out the TV.

The next day, we saddled up the horses and headed out to round up about sixty head of steers. We rode out through the rear of the barnyard and headed straight for the Crazies due west. We rode through two hayfields before crossing Sweet Grass Creek. As we crossed the creek, a sixty-foot bank rose nearly straight up. Our horses lunged out of the creek and onto the steep ground where they had to balance themselves on a game and cow trail weaving up the remainder of the steep climb.

Once up on the finger ridge, we rode slowly through the sparse trees. Vicky told me to stay out of the timber since I was an inexperienced rider. So I dropped down toward the fence line, making my way south on old Pard. Duane turned up to the higher ground, and Vicky moved right along the timber line. I slowly moved ten head toward the far southeast corner of the high country's fence line.

By the time I made it there, I had at least fifteen head. The cow dogs were with Vicky and Duane, and behind me, I could hear Vicky whistling, giving the dogs their commands. It felt like I was going to hold this little herd for longer than thirty minutes, so I swung my right leg over the horn of the saddle to shift some weight off my rear-end. I heard a lot of noise behind me and turned around to see what it was. Just then, old Pard shot out from under me and headed straight for a steer trying to run the fence line. I barely stayed in the saddle, and the last second flailing of my arms kept me from hitting the ground. I was amazed I had not lost my hat in this little rodeo and thankful that neither Vicky nor Duane had seen my skillful riding exhibition. I was thinking old Pard probably was dipping and turning to save my behind also.

Pretty soon, cattle and dogs were surrounding my little herd, and we pushed them all through the gate to the lower pasture. The horses knew their job was over and picked up the pace toward home. Duane saw lots of bear signs, and he thought for sure that bear wasn't going anywhere for a while. Turning north, the horses headed down the steep bank and came across the creek again, then stepped up on the dry ground bordering the barn yard. My legs and butt were pretty sore after a six hour ride.

About a week later, Vicky and Maxie had some business in Big Timber. Vicky told us, boys, to load up some salt licks and distribute them through five grazing pastures. That literally meant a day off, so we loaded our .22s and the salt licks and headed out right after breakfast. We started in the far north of the ranch in the "Big Field." We spent more time shooting gophers than actually setting the salt licks out. The more we shot, the more we kept talking about that bear.

Finally, we were in the south pastures, and behold! There was the bear above us, slowly heading toward the creek. He was rolling rocks over and eating his way north. We decided we could get him if we could just get in a position where he would be upwind from us. We ran up a small crease between two finger ridges to get above the bear. We thought that our best shot would be meeting him coming up the finger ridge, so picking out a knoll, we made our move. But the bear turned east and followed the gentle crease below us. Duane gave an animallike cry, "Ahh!" and the bear turned and looked at us. Duane aimed his .22, fired one shot, and the bear dropped like a ton of bricks. Adrenaline was still pumping through our veins from the long uphill run, trying to get ahead of the bear. I walked back to the Jeep and found a ditch to back it into, with the tailgate nearly level with the ground. The dead weight of the bear helped us to roll him downhill into the bed of the Jeep.

When we got home, we pulled the Jeep into the calving shed where there was a scale with a 350-pound limit. We attached the bear to it and pulled the truck slowly away. He broke the scale. When we skinned him, we saw that his maggot habit had ruined his hide. After the skinning, he looked like a human being, so to give tourists a scare, we propped him up for a week by a tree next to the creek, with a hat over his missing skull and a fishing pole between his hands. Our hunt turned disastrous when Vicky and Maxie made it home.

Vicky took our guns away and told us we could have both been killed. Then there was the issue of having no bear hunting license. The taxidermist told Vicky and Duane that he would have to order a bigger skull since this was one of the biggest bears he'd ever seen in these parts. He measured between the eyes to determine the skull size. We did get our guns back in a week but had to promise no more hunting safaris other than gophers.

A few months later, Vicky called me at home and told me how lucky we had been because the bear's ear canals were deformed into an oblong shape and were much bigger than normal. That was where Duane had hit him and killed him instantly. So Vicky wanted to remind me to thank God for saving our lives that day.

SWEET GRASS 8

You Stole My Car! No! I Had to See My Sweetheart!

The most regrettable thing I did on the ranch happened on a Friday night. Duane left to pick up his girlfriend, and Vicky, Maxie, Grandpa, and Grandma went to a luau at the Melville country school house. I really wanted to see my girlfriend, Sandy, and I decided to ask if I could use the Jeep to go to Livingston, and I drove to the luau to ask permission. When I arrived there, I found a big crowd sitting at many tables, but walking around looking for my boss or anyone else from the ranch, I could not find any. I thought it would probably be okay because Duane drove about the same distance to see his girlfriend on the other side of Big Timber.

I drove the Jeep over to the gas pump and started filling it up and then sat there for a while listening to this big argument going on inside me. I decided I should at least change my shirt, and before I could listen to any more reasoning, I was heading down the highway to Livingston. I don't remember what time I pulled up in front of Sandy's house on Sixth Street. After visiting with her folks for a while, we made our way to the piano on the front porch.

She was working on a piece for a big upcoming recital. I remember it was the theme song from the movie *Hush... Hush, Sweet Charlotte.* After a lot of unforgettable high school sweetheart hugs and smooches, I said my goodbyes and headed back to the ranch. The trip back seemed to be much more relaxed, and all the arguments had gone to bed. I pulled into the barnyard after 1:00 a.m. and went to bed reasonably happy.

Vicky woke me up the next day, but without his usual humor, "Let's get those cows milked this morning." Breakfast felt like I was at a mourning, and hardly a word was spoken besides a request to pass this or that. Suddenly, I realized I was going to lose my dream job today! Walking back to the welding shop with Duane, he broke the ice, "Jody, you pissed my dad off! I've never seen him this mad in all my life!"

At the welding shop, Vicky in a controlled but firm voice said, "You stole my vehicle last night! I was going to call the Highway Patrol, but I thought I'd give you until morning to see what you were thinking."

I started to tremble a little and every word that came to mind seemed inadequate. I finally just blurted, "I'm sorry, Vicky, I, I, I am sorry." I wanted to say, "I didn't think you'd mind," but "You stole my vehicle!" changed my mind, so my stuttering saved me from trying to justify my borrowing the car, not even to mention the tank of gas I took from his pump to drive to and fro.

Then Vicky said, "Why don't you guys mend the fence along the buffalo jump to the teepee rings on top."

So we grabbed some barbed wire and wire stretchers and headed over to the fence line that looked nearly vertical. I asked Duane, "Do you think your dad is going to fire me?"

"I really don't know. He's still pretty mad. That's why he sent us here. You know, he's removed all the keys from every vehicle, and that's definitely a first!"

So working seemed to be much better than any more rehashing how stupid I had been last night.

Lunch time came, and I thought of just going to the bunkhouse to start packing. Entering the mudroom though, I got the feeling I was forgiven, not by words but by a pat on the shoulder from Vicky. With some sense of relief, lunch tasted much better than the earlier sober breakfast. I felt I needed to say something, so I apologized, "I am sorry about the grief and worry I caused you by taking your Jeep last night. I don't blame you if you decide to fire me, but if you will give me another chance, I promise never to do that again."

Maxie spoke first, "Jody, if you miss home, we'll make arrangements so you can go home once in a while through the summer."

My mumble, "I wasn't missing home as much as I was missing my girlfriend," brought a few smiles around the table.

Then Vicky looked up from his plate after a slight pause and said in his sarcastic way, "No wonder Grease was moping around here this morning!"

That ended all my anxiety about being fired. Grandma quoted a verse from the Bible, "Surely goodness and mercy shall follow me all the days of my life, and I will dwell in the house of the LORD forever." Then with a smile, she looked at Maxie and said, "Let's clean up these dirty dishes!"

The load seemed to lift, and I felt I could have flown away to the highest snow-packed mountain peaks. There was never another word spoken about that incident for the rest of the years I worked there. As a matter of fact, they invited me to stay with them my junior year and go to high school in Big Timber. The politics around small-town sports affected varsity football, and I found myself warming the bench more than anyone would have expected. I was very grateful for such a good lesson in forgiveness. It made me realize they were treating me like family, not just another hired hand.

SWEET GRASS 9

Scrap Pile Miracles, Music, and a Mangled Rake

My memories of three summers at the ranch in my high school years are bundled together in time, but one thing stands out: Vicky was probably the smartest man I have ever met. That is still true today after my working for a utility company for thirty-seven years. The single illustration that describes it best starts with the pile of steel and iron by the door of the welding shop. Winter was the creative season for Vicky, and he made equipment like the "haystacker" out of a 1936 dump truck engine and frame. He fit it together with hydraulics and a boom with claws that reached into the hay wagon and transferred the hay from the wagon to the stack in eight scoops.

Once a reporter showed up with his camera; he interviewed Vicky, asking him where he had found the plans to build such an ingenious piece of equipment. Vicky smiled and tapped his index finger against the side of his head. The reporter looked incredulous and said, "You figured out all these hydraulics with no plans?"

Vicky simply answered, "I had a general knowledge of how hydraulics work." The truck engine worked in reverse, and the weight of the frame was suspended over the four rear wheels. Vicky painted it yellow.

Ranch life made running back and forth to the store very expensive due to loss of time and the cost of fuel. The greatest expense was time because you can never make up for lost time, so the metal scrap pile often became the hardware store. I was amazed over the years how many parts and other things could be made out of scrap metal.

During my first summer on the ranch, Vicky spent most of his time prepping for the coming haying season welding and mending the old pulling rakes. Actually, there were three identical rakes hooked together to form a larger swath of hay, raking it into bigger windrows. Every summer, Vicky said he hoped to make the old rake work for one more haying season.

My help around all this mending and welding was basically like that of a blind gopher, trying to learn where everything was in the shop. When I got tired of standing around, I leaned every once in a while on a freshly welded hot spot and got burned. I wish I could say that only happened once. The hitch system for the rakes aligned all three to be pulled in a straight line like a trailer. Once you got to where you were going to use them, you moved the two back rakes to the left to make a much wider swath. I think I helped do that maneuvering around just once.

Then came the day I was sent out to the hayfield to pull the rake back in for repairs. Vicky asked me to bring it back to the shop with the Jeep, so I went on my merry way with my sidekick Grease. We wheeled the Jeep around and hooked up the rake to the hitch. I set the radio up with a nice station out of Billings and slowly pulled out making sure all three rakes were behind the Jeep. I headed toward the lane's access gate, looked both ways like any safe driver would, and pulled into the lane. I suddenly heard an enormous sound of crushing metal, drowning out the radio. I got immediately out of the Jeep and saw the second rake mangled and wrapped around the wooden gate post. "Oh gee whizz!" This was going to be bad news.

I was trying to figure out what to do first when Vicky and Duane pulled up. Before I could open my mouth, Vicky hurriedly apologized, "Jody! This is my fault. I forgot to align the rakes before sending you out here to get them!" After assessing the damage, he said, "You know, whenever you're running machinery, you have to use your ears. And if something doesn't sound right or seems too loud, you need to stop and see what's going on." Then he pointed to my path, leaving the hayfield to the gate.

I had raked a wide swath all the way to the crash because I had not raised the rake's teeth up for transport. Talk about feeling stupid! Vicky raised his hand signaling me not to say anything, and he continued, "This is on me, Jody, but the good news is, you're forcing me to buy a new rake." The moral of the story is listening to good and loud music isn't always a good thing. It might make the scrap pile grow. Before the end of the day, he showed me how to use the oxygen/acetylene cutting torch.

In just a few days, the new wheel rake was delivered, and the dealer demonstrated how it all worked. The multiple large-wheeled disks had teeth moving hay from one disk to the next. The swath for this demonstration was just about eight feet wide, but Vicky wanted a much wider one. We eventually got the widest swath available in a single rake style, which was wider than the old configuration of three.

The ranch had four tractors; two were old English Fords with the insignia "Encore," and there were two smaller ones, a small Ford and a bigger one with a decal that read "Deluxe." The farmhand was attached to one of the Encores, and the smaller tractors had the mowing sickles attached at the rear. The normal routine was for the two tractors to work closely together in the same hayfield. It almost looked and felt like a race, and the deluxe tractor always beat the little Ford. Usually, Duane and I mowed together.

Once, when we were running behind schedule, Grandma and I mowed together, while Duane ran the farmhand, and Maxie and Sheryl drove the hay wagons back and forth to the corral. Sheryl, Vicky and Maxie's daughter had come home for a while because her husband had been sent to Vietnam. That gave me a reprieve from the dollhouse, and I moved into a wooden shed with a pot belly stove and an old iron bed.

Getting back to Grandma and me mowing, she did not understand the philosophy behind racing to mow the hay. I was right on her sickle tailgating the whole time. After getting the field mowed, I switched with Maxie and drove her hay wagon while she and Grandma went in to make lunch. At lunch, Vicky got an ear full of how I was trying to run over Grandma's sickle, and she was afraid for her life at my driving the tractor like a bat out of hell. Vicky grinned and asked, "Well, Jody, how did Grandma do today?" And Duane laughed and almost spit out a mouth full of food. Grandma then informed the table in a huff that she was mowing hay before we were born, and Grandpa added with his quiet voice and a big grin, "Are you bragging that you're never in a hurry to get it done?"

Grandma said with a shocked look on her face, "Well, we never broke anything back then, like these young guys. They are always fixing and welding!"

After a lot of conversing, giggling, and grinning, it was decided that Grandma and I were never to mow together again.

SWEET GRASS 10

Montana, Home of Hard
Heads and Big Hats

Montana has plenty of rodeos through the summer months, and there seems to be one in every nook and cranny of the state. The whole town looked forward to these cowboys' and especially the clowns' performances. Being raised in Montana, a rodeo meant summer was definitely here. And as a kid, it meant being in the rodeo parade, costume prizes, and games, in short—a big celebration!

Since the ranch was in the middle of nowhere, I never thought of rodeo season because all the posters and other hoopla in store windows were miles away from ranch life. So my first summer at the ranch, I was caught by surprise when I was invited to go to the Harlowton Rodeo this coming Friday and Saturday. That soon changed to excitement because we are cowboys working on a ranch for Pete's sake!

The more the subject came up, the more I understood that the Harlowton Rodeo wasn't a normal "big money" Rodeo. This was an amateur affair. As Vicky put it, "This is a real roundup rodeo with cowboys and animals flying through the air! It's not like those professional ones where maybe one cowboy gets bucked off, if you're lucky."

So the more I heard, the more it made for an eager anticipation. The two biggest ranches' names started coming up like this was a ranch versus ranch contest, with who had the best cowboys. It was basically the Colonel Stevens Ranch against the Cramer Ranch. To me, it seemed right out of an old Western cowboy movie.

That Friday, the fairgrounds were packed, and almost everyone there was in cowboy or cowgirl garb. I must say, my first impression was that this was real cowboy country. Vicky and Maxie hurried ahead, for they knew exactly where they wanted to sit. Duane and I were walking behind the chutes and livestock corrals, checking out the gates all the cowboys would be bucking out of. We studied the rigging and saddles and were fascinated by the variety of the gear of the different cowboys. Finally, we made it to Vicky and Maxie, high in the grandstands.

It started with the roping events, which were pretty much like every professional rodeo I'd ever been to. Then the announcer blared out the rider's and horse's names for the bareback event. There were about fifteen or twenty cowboys in the ring, and around the chutes these bucking broncos would be flying out of. The first bronco came out with a twist, and his back legs looked like he was trying to kick the moon. The cowboys in the ring were slapping the horse with their hats and were whooping and hollering at both horse and rider. It was like the Old West, I thought, and these guys were fearless. It was almost more interesting to watch the cowboys in the ring than the bucking show.

Some of the riders flew off the broncs in a matter of seconds after a chute opened and had terrible landings onto the arena. Two other men would come right over to offer a beer or a helping hand to get the bucked-off rider out of the ring. One rider wearing a ten-gallon Hoss Cartwright hat was hurled from his horse and landed head-first on the ground so hard that his hat was jammed over his eyebrows, bending his ears down to his earlobes. Two cowboys ran to his aid and started to pull the Bonanza icon up and off his head, but their efforts only lifted the cowboys butt off the dirt with every tug until the hat suddenly came off. The rescuers raised it up and swung it over their heads, and the laughter from the grandstands changed to a roaring cheer.

This was far from any rodeo I'd ever experienced. The saddle bronc event was similar to the bareback one. Then the announcer introduced the wild cow milking event, and two cowboys lined up, one with a bucket and the other with a lariat. Both were on foot, and when the wild cow was released, a chase as wild as the cow began. Tears were running down our faces from laughing so hard. I think that night, only one pair of cowboys was able to get a little milk out of one cow.

After that event, things got real serious with the announcement of the bull riding event. Vicky told us that last year, a bull broke through the fairground's fence and ran around the rodeo grounds. "That's why we sit here, on higher ground." All the cowboys in the ring suddenly disappeared, and two clowns rolled their barrels out. When that chute opened, there were flying cowboys and hats and bull snot like I'd never seen before. *Holy cow!* I thought, *These guys are completely nuts.* I can't believe that nobody went to the hospital or that no ambulance was needed to be rushed in to take one or two of these guys away. They were tough hombres for sure. No mention was made by the announcer about the fierce competition between the Colonel Stevens Ranch and the Cramer Ranch cowboys. It was probably only known and discussed behind the chutes.

The next day in the milking shed, Duane told his dad, "I'm going to enter the rodeo next year."

My mouth dropped open in shock, but Vicky said, "Well, Jody, what about you?"

I laughed and said, "Would this be for the wild cow milking event?"

And soon after a little burst of laughter, all you could hear was the distinct sound of milk squirting into the buckets. In the spring house, I asked Duane, "So what event are you thinking about entering next summer?"

"I'm thinking about the bull riding."

In a choking voice, I blurted out, "Really?"

"Yeah, Mom's brother John rode bulls professionally for a few years."

"You mean the John who raises sheep?"

"Yup, that's the John."

"Wow! I would've never guessed that."

"Yeah, he even rode once at Madison Square Gardens in New York."

"Wow! The home of Howard Cosell."

And he laughed, "Where do you come up with this stuff!"

"The milk shed, I guess. Blame it on the manure, but please don't tell Grandma."

"Just wait until dinner," Duane warned with a sarcastic laugh.

At dinner, I found out that no one was as surprised as me about Duane's plan to try his hand at bull riding. It was a crazy idea to me, but to everyone else at the table, it seemed simply a natural step. I felt like they must not have seen the same bull riding event at Harlowton that I saw!

The next week, John showed up for dinner. He had brought his rigging and spurs with him. At dinner, he explained how the bull's hide is what will throw you if you're not expecting all that shifting and moving of it. The spurs are really important, and they need to be dug into the bull's hide hard. As he talked more, questions were raised across the table; and after dinner, he said that he'd be more than happy to teach Duane everything he knew about bull riding.

News of this made it to Alex, Sheryl's husband, and soon John had two eager students. Suddenly, next year's rodeo became this summer's Three Forks Amateur Rodeo. A couple of milk cows became the practice bulls. One thing led to another, and rodeo talk took over the ranch's conversation. When the deadline for entry came up, Duane surprisingly decided not to enter, but Alex did. John and Duane spent a lot of time in the calving shed helping Alex get ready. They made a fifty-gallon barrel for a makeshift bucking bull with a couple of ropes and pulleys hanging from the ceiling. I even tried a couple of times to ride the barrel and immediately ended up dusting myself off.

The big day came, and Duane, John, and Alex made the long trip to Three Forks in Alex's Mach 1 Mustang. With chores and the normal ranch work filling our day, we looked forward to hearing all about the rodeo the next day.

The next morning, Vicky said that Duane watched Alex's chute opened and saw the bull run out without Alex. But whether Alex had jumped off or was bucked off at the same time the gate opened remains a mystery, since no one talks about it. With a laugh, he continued, "He at least rolled into the ring and tipped his hat to the crowd! But now, he's in a sling with a broken collar bone."

"Wow!"

"Wow is right, Jody, heck of a price to pay to hear an announcer say, 'Give Alex a big hand, folks!'"

And so, the rodeo frenzy came to a screeching halt that day.

SWEET GRASS 11

Do Cowboys Fly? Horses? Antelopes? Planes?

After the summers with these serious lightning storms and the loss of more than a dozen yearlings, Vicky made it a practice to go to the high country after a storm to check how the herd had weathered nature's electric peppering. Duane had some business in Big Timber, so it was just the boss and me saddling up the horses. It was common practice to walk them around a bit and check the cinch to make sure it was tight. You would hold the reins right by the horn of the saddle and make sure the horse's head was pulled down a little to his chest. Then you swung your right leg over and put your rear in the seat.

Everything seemed normal until I was sent flying over old Pard's head as soon as my butt hit the saddle. One of the strictest rules is that whatever happens, you never let go of the reins because that could mean a long, long, long walk home. I landed on my behind, flummoxed! Vicky laughed. "Did you check for a cocklebur under the saddle?"

I tried to smile but was too embarrassed and said in disgust, "Very funny, boss!"

"Just thank old Pard he bucked you off here instead of on some boulder!"

After slapping off my chaps and straightening out a few other things, I swung myself back up on old Pard, and it was like it had never happened.

We rode out the back of the barnyard at a slow pace. After going through the gate, we cantered along the road's ruts made by many vehicles traveling back and forth through the hayfields. We were side by side, talking and laughing, when all of a sudden, Vicky's horse, Chief, stumbled and did a somersault head over heels over Vicky. I knew right away Vicky was okay because he was cussing, and he never let go of Chief's reins. I dismounted to check out what in the world could have caused this now! We could not find anything, and Vicky said, "I think I'm in one piece, Jody."

"I see you are limping a bit!"

"Yeah, my ankle feels like it's sprained. Let's get out of here and get up to the high country."

We got to the creek before the big climb. Chief was drinking a lot of ice-cold creek water while Pard was blowing through his lips, swinging his head, and looking around. Vicky said, "Let's go, Jody!"

"Hey! Shouldn't we wait for Pard? He hasn't taken a drink yet."

"You've heard the saying, 'You can lead a horse to water, but you can't make him drink'?"

"Yeah, I have!"

"Well, Jody, now you've seen it firsthand!"

We made the climb up the steep bank and sauntered over the butte. Vicky wanted me to stay out of the timber again because that can get dangerous really quick. We rode through the herd and found all the animals in good shape. Before we got off the butte, we saw hundreds of antelope running below us five hundred yards away. For some reason, antelope never jump a barbed wire fence but go under it even though they could easily go over it. From that distance, the herd looked like water as they were running together and like waves as they went under the fences, truly a spectacular sight. We made our way back without any more incidents a couple of hours before dinner.

Unfortunately, Vicky's foot was so swollen he decided to go to the doctor in Big Timber. His sprained ankle turned out to be broken, and when he and Maxie made it home, one foot wore a cowboy boot and the other a cast. He was complaining about how long he would have to wear the cast and that his boot had to be cut off his foot. He was not a happy camper for sure. Vicky's accident with Chief was the first and last time I ever heard him cuss. I was amazed we had still finished the ride we had planned; it certainly seemed doomed from the start. But as Vicky once said, "If you're going to ride horses, you will be bucked off sooner or later."

A few days later, I was milking, and Duane went out to change the irrigation set. He returned a short time later, ran into the barn, and told his dad the irrigation ditches were dry. So after chores and breakfast, we drove up to the head water gate that was at the foot of the Crazies, right on the border of the National Forest.

We drove through a couple of gates, passed a little dammed reservoir, and turned to a steep climb that leveled out into a small clearing where we found several pickups parked with four cowboys standing by them. Two of them were carrying rifles. Vicky looked very serious and said, "Today, you're going to learn what it means to ride for the brand!"

My throat felt tight as we piled out of the Jeep. They turned out to be cowboys from Colonel Stevens Ranch, and they had shut down our water gate. Vicky talked to one of them, supposedly the foreman, and in a matter of minutes, we got into the Jeep again and headed back to the ranch. Vicky said in frustration, "Colonel Stevens hasn't heard of water rights before." He called the sheriff as soon as we got home and took another ride to the head water gate with the sheriff when he showed up. Vicky's ranch had water rights established back in the 1880s, and in a matter of hours, our irrigation ditches were full of water again.

Colonel Stevens's ranch was north of Vicky's. While irrigating one day, I was standing on a bit of high ground watching the water make its way downhill through the hay when I found out that the colonel was retired Air Force and had friends who put on air shows. All of a sudden, an F-4 Phantom roared overhead so close to the ground I instinctively ducked. The plane banked, traced the shape of the buttes, and did a couple of snap rolls before it broke the sound barrier and shot out of sight. It was like a mini air show and was repeated now and then when pilots felt like buzzing Colonel Stevens's place. I couldn't believe how low that F4 was to the ground and how it glided across the terrain making me feel like I was looking down at it. It was my private air show and one of the special moments irrigating brought without warning.

SWEET GRASS 12

Motorcycle Madness, a Ghostly Gallop, and a Crash

I've always been attracted to motorcycles. My first summer, my dad and two brothers came to the ranch to deliver my Suzuki 125 to me. Vicky let me move some cattle with it if I promised not to stampede them, so I enjoyed doing that a couple of times, but I liked it far better on horseback. Actually, the cow dogs could move the cows much more efficiently than me, but Vicky humored me by letting me use my motorcycle.

Jumping my motorcycle became a passion, but the chain tighteners took a beating and broke often, so my motorbike and I spent a lot of time in the shop. My goal was to jump over a barbed wire fence like Steve McQueen in *The Great Escape* but that goal was definitely a fantasy and was never realized. Since I am not mechanically inclined, Vicky and Duane became the mechanics who kept my bike running through the summer with all the abuse I put it through.

One night, I rode up to the Anchor Ranch and the National Forest for a change of scenery. Right after I started back, the old Suzuki died. I still had plenty of gas so I don't know why it quit. After giving it some thought, I decided to leave the bike behind and take the direct route across the fence lines, straight for the homestead. I was not sure how far away I was but thought it would take about an hour on foot. I started crossing the pastures, hayfields, and fence lines in a straight-line home.

Darkness fell, and I thought I was about halfway home. Soon, I could see the lights and yard lights down at the creek bottom. The horses up on the plateau looked like ghostly creatures in the light of the full moon. A dozen or more of them started getting frisky, trotting around and tossing their heads while circling at a distance. Then they came running at me at a full gallop. I froze in my tracks and was petrified at the thought they were going to trample me. When they were twenty or thirty feet away, they abruptly stopped, turned, and galloped away. When twelve or more horses are running toward you, the ground shakes. In spite of my fear, it was truly a beautiful sight under the full moon.

The following summer, I had a different motorcycle with me at the ranch, a Honda 175 Enduro I was practicing to jump with as high as possible out of a wide ditch. Friday night came around, and I decided I was going to drive to Livingston, about seventy miles southwest. I had ridden about five miles when the bugs became unbearable, and I decided to turn around and get my helmet. After I reached the city limits of Big Timber, I stopped to buy a couple of cans of oil. I figured by the time I got to Livingston, every store would be closed, so it made sense to get some oil just in case.

I tied the cans on the rack behind the seat and sped off to Livingston. At night, I always felt safer because I was more visible to cars than in the daytime. Just east of Springdale, a gust of wind hit me, and I turned to feel behind me for the cans of oil. Before I could turn back, a car started passing me on the right, inches away from my handlebar. Then in slow motion, I was pulled in between the car's trunk and a trailer. I fell, and as my head lay on the white shoulder line of the highway, I saw a green single-wheeled trailer and car come up through the ditch and make it back onto the shoulder of the highway. Two people came running toward me. I was able to make it to my feet before they reached me. My motorcycle's light was shining straight up from the center divider line. The anxious couple asked me, "Are you okay? Where are you going?" Then they handed me my wallet and a bunch of papers, all this in slow motion. I asked them to get my motorcycle out of the middle of the highway, and the man rolled it into the ditch and up on the kickstand. They then asked me again, "Are you sure you're okay?"

"Yeah, I'm okay."

They hurried back into their car and drove away.

Back in the sixties, the highways in Montana did not have very much traffic, so I crossed the highway and decided to hitchhike back to Big Timber. The first thing I noticed was that my pants from the back pocket to the back of my knee were torn wide open. Also, my right thumb was not in any shape to be used to hitch a ride. I saw a set of headlights coming my way and, using my left thumb, flagged it down. Thank God, the car pulled over and picked me up. I could smell the two guys in it were drunk, but beggars can't be choosers. I told them I needed to get to the hospital in Big Timber. They were sympathetic to my plight and took me straight to the front door.

The nurse on duty knew Vicky and was familiar with his family ranch outside of Melville. After an x-ray, they put my right hand in a cast. I had crushed my little finger's knuckle. I called my folks in Livingston, but they weren't home. So I called Vicky, and in about an hour, Maxie and Vicky showed up. Vicky called the Highway Patrol, and they came from three different directions looking for the car with the green wooden single-wheeled trailer. The Highway Patrol supervisor called and told Vicky he thought I was lying. Vicky defended me as my own father would have, and I respected him for that.

I finally got hold of my folks, and my mom especially wanted me to come home. When I asked Vicky if he could use a one-handed hired hand, he assured me I could stay on for the summer. A few days later, my right knee was giving me trouble. It was swollen, and I could hardly bend it. I rested it for a while and then found a steep path to run up and down to loosen it up. I wasn't going to let that knee screw up the upcoming football season.

SWEET GRASS 13

The Andersons, a Kind Priest, and the Sabbath

My mother had made sure from the beginning I would attend the Catholic church every Sunday, and because Vicky's family attended the Melville Lutheran Church close by, Vicky and Maxie made arrangements with a family to take me to Big Timber to church with them. They had a small dairy farm, and on their huge red barn was painted a large white *A* for Anderson.

The first time I was to go to church with them, I drove the old Wagoneer Jeep to their place about five miles east. I arrived early Sunday morning, and Mrs. Anderson answered the door and invited me in while they were getting ready. Vicky had told me they had a daughter about my age named Kate, and apparently, we were waiting for her. When she appeared, we hurried to their car and I sat in the back seat. There was the normal small talk about what was going on at our different ranches and how everyone was doing health-wise. Mrs. Anderson's husband was doing the milking, and I learned that was the normal schedule on Sunday. Kate and her mother looked very much alike. From the back seat, their jet-black hair looked to even be curled exactly the same. Kate was a husky outdoorsy-looking girl, who seemed very quiet compared to her mother. We arrived at the Big Timber Catholic Church and parked down the street because the parking lot was already full, though when we hurried in to Mass the church was only half full.

I recognized the priest right away as the Polish priest for whom dad and I had laid carpet last summer. I couldn't recall his name but remembered we were shocked that he had already moved all the furniture out of the front room by the time we got there. Then his housekeeper fixed a really nice meal for us at lunch. What stood out in my mind was that he asked dad if it was okay with him if we had ice cream with wine for dessert. Dad said yes, and we were served vanilla ice cream, and the housekeeper poured as much wine over it as we liked. The priest told us this is the way they serve ice cream in Poland. Both dad and I enjoyed it although I could not tell you what kind of wine it was. The memory of that job and how nice both the priest and his housekeeper were made church a bit more interesting, as did the words rolling off his tongue in a very Polish accent.

After Mass, Mrs. Anderson was chatting with a few acquaintances and friends on the sidewalk, and Kate hung by her mother's side and seemed to enjoy the conversation. In a small town like Big Timber, no one ever locked their car, let alone take the keys out of the ignition, so I walked back to the car and climbed into the backseat again. The ride home was quiet with some finger-pointing here and there to comment on a little history or a place where they knew the family who lived there.

My first Sunday on the ranch was surprisingly quiet. Maxie had told me the night before to help myself to lunch or dinner. I found some fried chicken in a bowl and ate by myself. This first Sunday seemed very strange to me because no one was around. Maxie had left a note in case I forgot where everything was. Even the dogs seemed to be in this quiet rest mode hanging over the ranch on Sundays. About the only activity was milking, and at about five in the afternoon, the dogs had the cows rounded up and waiting at the milk shed's door. Duane and Vicky emerged from their hiding places, and we milked the cows as we had that morning.

Then the kidding started, with Duane's comment, "Well, I guess you will be going to the Anderson's more than on Sundays now. You know the saying about the family that prays together stays together?"

Then Vicky offered his observation, with a laugh, "That Kate can throw a bale of hay as well as any guy can, Jody!"

Duane added, "You might want to start doing a few pushups before you date her."

And so every Sunday I went to church with the Andersons, I was kidded about Kate from a different angle. For the three summers of traveling to and from church with Kate and her mother, we discussed the weather and how the hay was doing that particular year and not much else of interest. Duane, in a serious moment, told me that he and Kate were in the same grade and rode back and forth on the school bus from Melville to Big Timber.

The family at Sweet Grass observed the Sabbath on Sundays, and every seventh year, they rested their fields as God had instructed farmers to do in the Old Testament. They rotated the grazing pastures to rest the grass through the summer. Vicky once said, "If I took care of my ranch like the government takes care of Yellowstone Park, I wouldn't have a ranch." We never left wire, nails, or any other debris on the ground, and I learned they were diligent about everything on the ranch except at that shooting gallery by the lane. I often wondered why the gophers had not moved away from there a long time ago.

SWEET GRASS 14

Some Doctoring, Skunks, Bubble Baths, and Frisky Bulls

Vicky did all his own doctoring of the cattle, horses, and dogs. What we came to call "hoofrot" was caused by flies in hot summers. When we saw a cow or bull limping or hobbling around, we roped the head and hind hooves and stretched the animal out between two vehicles until it lay flat on the ground, and we were able to administer the prescribed medication, which came in a needle and a syringe. You also had to force the needle in by pounding on the hide with your fist to get the needle to penetrate. Then you screwed the syringe onto the needle to push the medicine into the animal. How often this had to be done depended on the weather, because one summer you might have to doctor three or four animals, and another at least a dozen or more.

We were in the far north pasture administering "hoofrot" medicine to a cow. After removing the ropes from her, she staggered off toward the rest of the herd. We had just started piling into the Jeep when a coyote appeared out of nowhere. With Grease and me in the bed of the Jeep, the race was on. We chased it to the fence line where there was a stand of wheat. Grease and I got down and followed the coyote's trail through the wheat, running as fast as our legs could carry us. Suddenly, I heard Grease let out a blood-curdling yelp! Before I could stop, I was in a misty cloud that took my breath away. We had run right into a healthy skunk, and it was all we could do to get out of that cloud so we could breathe. Vicky and Duane were watching the whole incident from across the fence line next to the trail we thought we were on. They were a hundred yards away and could smell us. When we got close to the Jeep, Vicky said painfully, "Jody, you and Grease in the back!"

When we got back to the mudroom, I stripped outside and went directly into the tub. My nose still burned from the stench, and it seemed like that was all I could smell. Duane got me some clean clothes and threw them on the bathroom floor, saying with tons of sarcasm, "Jody! You'll want to take another bath, or you'll have to eat with the dogs tonight!"

Grandma yelled from behind the door, "There's some smelly bubble bath on the shelf behind you, Jody. It's in a purple bottle, try that!" After a few moments, she yelled again, "I wish we had tomato juice right now!"

So I drained the tub and started over. Unfortunately, the purple bubble bath did little to remedy the smell. At dinner, a lot of sniffing sounds told me how much I actually still reeked of skunk, and it lingered for a long time afterward. Grease and I were banned from the cabs of all vehicles for a week or more.

Another time, we went after a Charolais bull that needed treatment. We herded the old fellow onto some flat ground, and Vicky and Duane were on foot to rope the head and heels. Duane hit a bullseye with his lasso. After a couple of tries, Vicky managed to loop both hind legs and tie them to the front bumper of the Jeep. I slowly backed the Jeep up, and Vicky raised his hand signaling all was secure. The bull was fighting his predicament, rocking and rolling and pawing with his front legs. Vicky made his way up from the animal's spine side, staying away from his hooves. With a quick jab and push of the syringe, the medicine was administered.

My thoughts now turned to how in the world we were going to get the ropes off this huge angry creature. I was thankful I was in the driver's seat and pulled the Jeep slowly forward. The rope came off the heels, and the bull sprang to his feet. Luckily, the medicine isn't an instant cure because he hobbled up, favoring his front hoof. He turned to give his head a shake, Duane flicked his lariat, and it spun right off like he knew what he was doing. The bull seemed to understand this was meant to help him, and we were soon heading for the shooting gallery to calm down after a lot of excitement and the instant adrenaline rush.

The ranch had one Charolais bull, three Angus bulls, and three Herefords, with over two hundred head of cows. Vicky figured a bull should be able to impregnate about thirty cows through the summer. During my three summers there, I only remember having to administer "hoofrot" medicine to the Charolais. Vicky once said, "You can't keep up with the bulls when you set them out to pasture, and you then have to whip them into the winter corral. About two hundred calves in spring are good news for a rancher's pocketbook."

SWEET GRASS 15

Of Haying, Calving, Branding, and Long Days!

The hay corral was located at the entrance of the barnyard just off the county road. The entry and exit gates were wide enough to pull a set of dual hay wagons straight into the corral. Vicky's invention made short work of unloading them as the hydraulically controlled claws of the stacker grabbed the hay and lifted it on the stack. The haystack when finished looked like a huge loaf of bread. When the tractor that had the farmhand mounted on it came in, we climbed on its forks, and Duane would lift us to the top of the stack.

Vicky called the job on top "roofing" the haystack, and with pitchforks, we moved the loose hay around to fill any holes in the stack. Usually, it was an easy job, but once in a while, we needed more hay and, with a lot of pitchfork work, filled a gaping hole. Vicky and I had done this job together more than any other job on the ranch, and we had some serious conversations while working.

One particular talk was generated by the threat of a nuclear holocaust. Vicky told me that he too once carried around that fear but was liberated from it when he learned that God would be the One to destroy the world, not man. I know, out of all those conversations on the haystacks, I still carry that one with me for more than fifty years now.

The book of Revelation in the Bible says in chapter 11:18 (ESV): "The nations raged, but Your wrath came, and the time for the dead to be judged, and for rewarding Your servants, the prophets and saints, and those who fear Your name, both small and great, and for destroying the destroyers of the earth." I found this years later, and amazingly, it still gives me comfort today.

Vicky's philosophy behind the loose stacks was all about saving work and time in the end. He also thought that in winter feeding, it was much easier to distribute the loose hay than handling traditional bales. Something I also never caught was that the Western TV series *Bonanza* used baled hay instead of loose. That was a mistake because the series was set in the 1800s before baling became a practice.

Occasionally, I went out to the ranch in mid-March for a week to help them with calving. *Helping* is probably the wrong term because usually, it was more observing. Every couple of hours, we'd check and make sure the cows were birthing without a problem. After breakfast, we'd saddle up the horses and ride out to what was called the winter pasture. You'd ride through the herd and find all the cows that had a half hitch in their tail, which indicated they were close to birthing, and you'd push them into a group. The cow dogs would hold the herd together while you looked for those who were ready to drop their calf. Quite often, you'd find a cow with a calf that had been dropped during the night. One time, we watched a cow giving birth on a snowbank and saw the calf sliding off it. Wow! The little guy had the thrill of greeting this cold world and going down a slide all at the same time!

After gathering these ladies up, we'd push them out into the lane and mosey them toward the barnyard at the homestead. Once in a while, there was an angry mom who did not want to go along with the others, but the cow dogs were great herders, and the cow was met with a dog's relentless herding instinct. It definitely was a better idea and a lot nicer to go with the flow than fight a couple of dogs nipping at your heels.

One night, a cow was giving birth, but her calf was turned tail-first instead of headfirst. Vicky reached in to try to turn the little guy, but he couldn't, so we ended up pulling the calf out the wrong way. Afterward, the mother didn't want anything to do with it and refused to let it suck. So Vicky brought around a mother whose calf had died earlier, and when he wiped her afterbirth on the ousted calf, she let the little guy suck. You learn quickly how every cow has its own personality just like people. The calving season has a lot of drama with life and death scenes woven through it. It's very exciting and also sometimes very sad. Vicky told me point-blank, "Every calf is about two hundred dollars won or lost, that's how you have to look at it." I have to say that, for me, calving was the most exciting time on the ranch.

Branding was a big job, and because of high school, I normally missed it, but once I took time off to take part in this cowboy roundup. The smell of burning rawhide is the first telltale sign you're at the right place. Also amazing is the noise mothers and calves make when they are separated, and the din is a nonstop affair. The male calves' testicles are rubber banded, every calf is vaccinated, and two hundred head of cattle are branded. Neighbors come to help because the sheer numbers are too much for any one rancher to handle in one day.

I know TV and Hollywood have made branding something glamorous, with roping and horses and cowboys showing off all their buckaroo skills. But branding here was grabbing a calf and throwing it down, or just plain tackling it, then holding it down for three other fellows to quickly do all that had to be done to the squirming little guy. You employed your knee and all your weight to pin down your charge.

Vicky liked to do it when they were young so you would not have to try holding down a hundred-pound calf. The job was a bit bloody because we would also notch the calf's left ear, which enables you to see its identity with just a turn of the head. Branding made for a long physically exhausting day for all the two- and four-legged participants.

SWEET GRASS 16

An Overdressed Roadrunner, a PC Party, and a Do-si-do

After finishing haying early in August 1970, Vicky had me start irrigating for a second crop the same day. The next day, he came with me; and together, we moved and set our canvas dams and were watching the water slowly moisten the stubbles of the hayfield. We hardly ever saw any kind of traffic on the county road that bordered our fence. The road made a perfect *T* that paralleled and intersected the ranch's two big sections, the stem of the *T* running east and west and the crown of it north and south. To the north, there was a town famous only for its peculiar name, "Two Dot Montana." The south portion was less inviting, running past two ranches and dead-ending at the National Forest Service land.

While we were taking a break from our labor, we saw a cloud of dust rolling up along the road. Before we could get out, "What's that guy's hurry?" a maroon-and-black Plymouth Road Runner turned through our open pasture gate. Vicky left his shovel and headed down, sloshing through the hayfield. The Road Runner stopped, and the driver, who was dressed in a suit and tie, waved like he knew he had reached his destination. While I was watching in bewilderment, wondering, *Who in the world would come out to an irrigated hayfield dressed like that?* I heard Vicky shout in his booming voice, "Welcome home!"

After a big hug, the two men disappeared from view. I heard Vicky's loud laugh and saw them stand up and brush themselves off, both laughing hysterically. Obviously, they knew each other, and that greeting was the wildest hello I've ever experienced. The mysterious dark suit departed, and Vicky slowly walked back toward me while the Road Runner was making a twelve-point *U*-turn and retraced its tracks to the county road, disappearing out of sight in another large cloud of dust.

Vicky had mud on his cheek and a big grin on his face. His jeans were wet and muddy, and he had a patch of mud between his shoulder blades. I could hardly control myself, "So what was all that about?"

"Jody, that kid was once the student body president of the University of Montana! And it's the first time I've seen him in about three years."

"Wow! So he is a wrestler from the college?"

Vicky said with a smirk, "Nobody comes out to these pastures in a suit and tie and leaves without a little dirt on them! He came to invite us to a Peace Corps party at that abandoned dude ranch east of Anderson's place. They've trained a bunch of city slickers, and now these kids are headed for Ecuador."

"Wow! How does that work?"

"I guess America doesn't realize those farmers in Ecuador know what they are doing. They've only been farming for centuries down there. Kind of crazy, don't you think?" Vicky paused to shake the mud off his back. "I think these kids will be trained by those Ecuadorian farmers."

"So when is the big hoedown?"

"Next Saturday night!"

"Oh, good! I'll still be here!"

Vicky sarcastically added, "I wouldn't get too excited, Jody! I don't think Grease has ever been to a dance."

We laughed as we threw our shovels over our shoulders and headed for the Jeep.

The Peace Corps was John F. Kennedy's brainchild. It sent volunteers all over the world to provide international assistance to disadvantaged nations. I remember seeing a host of commercials about the Peace Corps and thought it would be interesting to see these kids up close and personal.

Saturday night rolled around, and I told Vicky I'd drive us there in my old 1956 Mercury. As soon as we were off with Maxie and Vicky in the backseat, I heard Maxie slap Vicky's thigh and say in a scolding tone, "Stop being funny, or I am going to ride up front with Jody!" I turned around to see Vicky's face turn red and said to myself, *Now, that's something you don't see every day.*

We pulled into the abandoned dude ranch and noticed its buildings still looked rather overgrown with weeds. Vicky said with a puzzled expression, "I wonder where they are farming around here?"

A lot of local families had come to the party, and the Peace Corps had set out a big bowl of punch and desserts of almost every kind. Vicky's wrestling buddy introduced the twelve guys and gals who were headed for Ecuador. They all told a story of why they had decided to volunteer for the Peace Corps. Most came from large cities across the States, had never been in the country, and all had had to find their own way to Melville, Montana. It was interesting to hear their stories and that they couldn't believe they were so far out in the middle of nowhere.

I kind of kept my eye on Vicky and jokingly asked, "Are you two guys going to wrestle again?"

Vicky said, "No way! I only wrestle in wet hayfields!"

His wrestling partner overheard him and laughed. Then the record player started up, calling out squares for square dancing. So almost everyone started dancing. My specialties, do-si-do and promenade, really showed off my two left feet, and my left and right arms became confused about where to go. Yes, I truly showed those Peace Corps city slickers how we square-dance in Montana. Poor Maxie was laughing so hard she had to sit down to catch her breath, and Vicky asked, "What punch bowl are you drinking from? No wonder Grease didn't want to come!"

When I had finished my demonstration, we promenaded out of there.

Back in the old Merc, we headed back to the homestead. Once I got going with tomfoolery, it was hard to return to a level of somberness. The old Merc had a low-beam headlight out, but both high beams worked fine. I told Vicky and Maxie I would *strobe* them home and started blinking the dimmer switch on and off. Just before we dropped down to the creek bottom, a car approached us, but I kept strobing my headlights. The driver put out his hand to signal a stop, so I stopped, and since it was summer, of course, our windows were down. The driver acted like he didn't notice my strobing headlights while I had thought he was going to tell me I must have a bad short or something. But no, he asked me for directions to a ranch I had never heard of. So I told him, "Wow! What a coincidence, we're looking for the same place you are!" With that, both Maxie and Vicky started laughing uncontrollably. The guy pulled away with a look that said, "Drunker than a skunk," and we turned into the ranch. I headed for bed and was still laughing when my head hit the pillow.

SWEET GRASS 17

Two Dot Montana and Uncommon People

One summer, we had to whip an injured bull into the barnyard all the way from the pasture to be loaded up in the holding corral. After that, we watched Duane's roping exhibition where he missed looping his high dollar lariat around his saddle horn and was pulled off his horse. And all you could see was a cowboy hat chasing a runaway yearling through the tall grass. We eventually got Duane's rope off the yearling, and he was able to pull the grass from his chaps and dig the dirt out of his belt buckle. These incidents led Vicky to consider that building another holding corral and loading chute closer to the grazing pastures would be a good idea. Once he decided where it was going to be, he did a lot of measurements and figured out how much material would be needed.

When I worked with my dad, we would head to a lumberyard or hardware store when we needed material. On the ranch, it was a little different. We got a pole trailer ready and fueled up the brand-new four-wheel drive Ford pickup. Even before that, I had heard a lot of talk about the Little Belt Mountains having the perfect lodge-pole pines. They were the straightest lumber around and would make perfect poles and rails for a new corral, and I was finally going to see this legendary place named Two Dot Montana. We'd have to drive through the place to make our way to the Little Belts.

One morning, Vicky had read a very good article in the Billings Gazette having to do with the Hutterites, and he was so interested in it that he read a large portion of it out loud at breakfast. In the article was the shocking information that the Hutterites would pay men to impregnate their women because they were having inter-relational marriage problems.

Our trip to the Little Belts would lead us right by the Hutterites Colony, and Vicky said, "I'll be more than happy to drop you off and pick you up on the way back, Jody!" The subject stirred up a lot of jokes and kidding. A few days later, a truck pulled up at the ranch, and there were the Hutterites selling vegetables. We knew who they were because they were all dressed in black. We were in the welding shop and heard their vehicle pull up. Of course, Vicky immediately came up with, "Hey, Jody! The Hutterites are here to pick you up!"

I was about to faint when I heard what he said and was thankful to hear the burst of laughter coming from Duane and Vicky, who were unable to hold it in. I think every pore of my body excreted a large drop of moisture, and my knees were buckling. Vicky sank his hook in a little deeper with, "You know, Jody, when I called them about you, they said you sounded like a perfect candidate!"

In relief, I slapped my thigh and ignored his comment with my signaled no-way grin, and Vicky's, "Gee, I was just trying to help a friend!"

And I couldn't hold back my "With a friend like that, who needs enemies?"

We ended up laughing at one another and returned to what we were doing when that vehicle pulled up beside the kitchen where Maxie bought a fresh crate of vegetables.

I did get to drive through Two Dot Montana, and we passed by the Hutterites Colony with Vicky giving me an elbow nudge, "Last chance now?" And without a word, I folded my arms and just smiled. Then in about five minutes, Duane commented, laughing, "Jody! I thought you were going to pass out the other day. You should have seen your face!"

Then we all started laughing.

"Yeah, Duane, your dad really got me on that one!"

We pulled up in the National Forest of the Little Belts and surveyed the lodgepole pines. It looked like they were only standing a foot from one another, but close up, they were probably three or four feet apart. Vicky and Duane cut about a dozen or more poles down. We had a little picnic for lunch and started loading the poles up on the trailer. I have to agree, they were about the straightest ones I've ever seen.

We managed to make it back in time for milking, and I got to drive through Two Dot twice. Just for the record, there were three houses by the roadside, and one of them was a saloon. I guess every town in Montana has a watering hole. That's something my dad always said. Not sure how true that is, but Two Dot Montana had its own watering hole, that's for sure.

SWEET GRASS 18

Water Polo, Potatoes, a Hunt, and a Man Named Joe

During haying season, we all worked hard and put in long days in the rush to get the hay off the field. It also was normally the hottest time of the year. Vicky had dug a cylindrical hole with a diameter of eighteen to twenty feet and lined it with black plastic to make a swimming hole, about six feet to the right of the dollhouse porch. It also had a diving board, but only cannonballs were safe to do because the sides tapered quickly to the center and deepest point, and you had to keep your arms out in front to dive. Actually, water polo cowboy style was the main attraction. But the refreshing dip was a welcome comfort after a hot and dirty day in the hayfields. The pool also attracted neighbors on those very hot summer days.

When the pool was refilled with water from the springhouse, it normally took at least a week until you could tolerate the ice-cold water enough in hopes to get used to it. This rugged cowboy pool wasn't for the faint of heart. Because the sides were so slanted and steep, it was easy to slip or slide back into the center of the pool. But no one ever complained, nor was there an accident that I ever heard of. I just remember a lot of yelling and some good old competition from the best cannonballs to the best water polo team. Among my fondest memories is Vicky's knack for making even the hardest work fun one way or another.

Probably the worst memory of chores on the ranch is weeding the potato patch, called "the penance patch," which was about a hundred by fifty feet and looked to be twenty rows of nothing but potatoes. I was assigned the unpleasant job of pulling the weeds in it. It often felt like pulling weeds along the side of an endless highway somewhere in Nevada. It was a hand-and-knee operation, crawling down each row to pull those endless weeds. I learned this was a good place to use your imagination and an even better place to pray that God would never again allow another weed to even think of planting itself among these potatoes.

I didn't mind flood-irrigating the potato patch, but weeding was a chore that I lamented all day. The penance patch was about a hundred yards outside the back gate in a clearing close to Sweet Grass Creek and was surrounded by cottonwoods forming a natural fence around the patch. After the potato harvest, the patch rested until the afternoon spring sun warmed the soil to plow and plant for the next harvest. I never got to enjoy the harvesting chore because I left the ranch by the last two weeks in August for football, but Maxie would remind me the following summer, "These potatoes on the table are the ones you cared for and weeded last summer." It usually took me at least two rows to stop pouting over the horrible job it was. I guess it had become therapy by the time I was done since I tried to be as thorough as possible in hopes that it would be a long time before having to return to do penance again. One consolation was that the potato patch had the softest dirt ever, and it was easy on my knees, which, of course, is very important to a teenage quarterback.

When I was a kid, hunting was a big deal. The male attendance at high school dropped by about two-thirds the first week of deer hunting season, and on the morning of the season's opening, almost every restaurant and cafe in Livingston was filled with red-coated hunters. One time, Dad asked me to get permission from Vicky to come up and hunt on his ranch. After Vicky's okay, Dad invited his oldest brother to come along with his boys, which ticked me off because I felt my dad was taking advantage of Vicky's hospitality. We arrived on the ranch with seven hunters, and two friends of his sister in California came along as well.

Vicky had told me a few stories about a man his dad had hired when he was a kid. He referred to him as "Indian Joe." And you could tell Vicky had enormous respect for "Indian Joe" and for his knowledge and experience with the wild and the creatures that live there. We went out with a dozen hunters in three four-wheel drive vehicles and climbed the butte east of the winter wheat field. Then we parked the vehicles and climbed the rest of the butte on foot. Vicky explained to everyone that the deer would come out into this clearing, and we were to stay as quiet and still as possible so we would be able to get a nice shot. His only requirement was to please make sure it's at least a two-point buck.

Then Vicky and I started in a half run off the top of the butte and back to where the vehicles were parked and then farther down-hill toward the north and the "big field." In this trot, we rounded the base of the butte and then turned east again. Vicky stopped and explained we would move up into the timber from here, and the deer would run into the guys we left behind. We moved uphill in more of a walk, not really hunting, with the idea of pushing the game into an ambush.

About a third of the way up, we heard gunshots coming from the top. By the time we got there, eight of the guys that we left behind had shot a deer. After dressing the deer out, we dragged them back to the trucks. The hunters all took pictures of their trophies. One of my cousins had shot a yearling that had no horns, and Vicky made him also take a picture with his trophy. Although I could tell Vicky was upset about what had happened, he joked in a sarcastic way to appear to be more of a good sport about the bad shot. Then Vicky grabbed me and said, "You and I are going to the high country."

While driving toward the National Forest, Vicky asked me, "Do you think you can keep up with the old man?"

"I think so." I didn't mention that I was in good shape because of football season, which had just finished a couple of weeks ago. I learned from the race with Duane that you never count your chickens until they are hatched.

We went through a couple of gates and pulled the truck up to a dead end. In a quick trot or half run, we started up a well-worn game trail. After a good ten-minute uphill jog, Vicky raised his hand, and we came to a complete stop. He pointed to the clump of trees above us and whispered, "See the fur!"

My eyes couldn't believe he could see that patch of fur between the bark of those trees. Then he said hurriedly, "Let's go!"

We did another long sprint, and we were up and out of the timberline and onto a finger ridge. Another ridge was about a hundred yards away. Vicky said immediately, "That old boy is going to come out between those two boulders, so take a deep breath and squeeze one off!"

I had no more got down and aimed when this huge buck appeared where Vicky said he would. Vicky whispered, "Now, Jody!"

I fired, and the shot echoed.

Vicky smiled at me. "Jody! You missed!"

"Wow! I think I was high, huh?"

"Well, if anyone asks, we'll say you scared him to death. We have to go now."

We traced our trail down to the truck, now running the whole way to beat nightfall.

Driving back to the ranch as our headlights lit the way, I felt almost holy like I had touched the holy grail of "Indian Joe." I think he is the reason at the ranch I was never called "Joe." Because there, his name hung in the hall of fame in each one's mind. It was something they all honored in a private and personal way. And the few stories I heard made me feel privileged to have caught a glimpse of "Indian Joe."

SWEET GRASS 19

About Shepherds, Heroes, a Fox, and a Fearless Friend

Very noticeable on the south and west buttes were these large stacks of rocks that looked like pillars. They piqued my curiosity, so I asked Vicky about them, and he told me they were pillars the shepherds built while tending their sheep, and there was a competition going on as to the height and stability of each man's stack. These pillars were making a statement as if they were shouting, "Look up here, at us!" I don't know how tall they were or which was the highest, but they were visible from a long distance looking south and west.

One day around lunchtime, we heard an urgent knock on the mudroom door. When Vicky opened it, a bald, disheveled-looking man whose face was covered with large dark warts with little horns protruding from them came in and asked to use the phone. He explained in a soft voice that his sheep were dying from what he thought might be poisonous grass, and he needed to call a vet. Maxie invited him in, pulled up a chair, and told him to eat with us, but he explained he had left the sheep alone with the dogs and needed to get back before nightfall.

He obviously had a heart for his sheep and went to great lengths to care for them. He reminded me of King David in the Bible, who was a shepherd before he became the most famous king of Israel. He defended his sheep from wild animals, rescuing a lamb from the mouth of a lion, and another one from a bear by prying the bear's jaws apart. I was relieved our shepherd left though because he was hard to look at with that damaged face. He was the only man I ever met out of those who built the pillars on the buttes.

Also interesting to see were the small private planes circling the huge horseshoe formed by the buttes. They were coyote hunters that often came humming overhead, casting their shadows across the landscape. I don't know if there was a bounty on coyotes there or not, but the planes were searching for prey.

One summer, I arrived to start work again; and one morning Vicky wanted to show me a fox pup he and Duane had rescued from a damaged den. He pulled on a long nylon rope, and out from under the mudroom came this fox pup. Vicky picked him up and said jokingly, "We trained this fox, and he's a pretty quick learner." He stretched out the leash as far as it could go. Then he said, "Don't blink, or you'll miss his trick." He set the fox down, and in a flash, he raced back to the mudroom again, and out of sight, his tail gracefully floating behind him as he tucked into his temporary den.

In about a week, there was still no improvement as to tricks, and Vicky let him go. A couple of times when I was irrigating, I saw him watching me from only about a hundred feet away. I told Vicky about it, and he thought the little guy was just domesticated enough to get himself shot by hanging out too close to people.

My last summer on the ranch, I learned my beloved Grease had been shot in her hind quarters, and she was never the same after that. Vicky was pretty upset that a hunter had shot his dog. But he's had cows shot as well during hunting season. The following winter, Vicky let me know that Grease had died in her sleep. She was the first real hunting dog that I had been around, and she had a lot of personality. She was part Airedale and part Chesapeake Bay Retriever, and her coat was curly and rust-colored. She was named Grease because she liked to chew on greasy rags when she was a pup. She loved to go irrigating with me and chase down all the different creatures escaping the floodwaters. At times when the hay was tall, you could only see the tip of her tail. To me, she seemed not only fearless but also smart when it came to chasing down some dangerous animal, hightailing it out of the flood.

SWEET GRASS 20

Sweet Grass Revisited

About ten years after my last high school summer on the ranch, I returned for a visit, now with my wife and two children. The gateway to my fond memories was opened by the sight of the Melville Church as soon as I turned off the highway, much as it was the first time when I turned up this lane with Grandma. It was different in that back then, I was nervous and kind of anxious, not knowing what to expect. It is funny how your mind writes its story out in a narrative that becomes a part of you.

We dropped off the plateau toward the familiar bridge and then turned in to cross the cattle guard through the barnyard, appearing the same in a timeless setting. I noticed right away there were no geese or chickens hurrying out of the way, no milk cows calmly watching us motoring past, and no horses in sight either. A different breed of cow dogs ran along beside the car barking the alarm that a stranger is here. The kitchen door opened, and Vicky and Maxie met us with big, warm smiles. A very inviting-looking lunch was waiting for us on the familiar worn table. After they met my little family, we started remembering and sharing some old stories and adventures, and the big laughs were soon ringing across the table just like in the old days.

During the three summers I had lived and worked with him and the family, Vicky had become like a second dad to me, and I had come to respect and love him as I did my own dad. After lunch, he was eager to take me around to show me the pastures and also the hayfields where I could not believe the size and numbers of the haystacks after a bumper crop that summer. As the parable of the growing seed in Mark 4:26–27 says: "This is what the Kingdom of God is like: night and day, whether he sleeps or gets up, the seed sprouts and grows, though he does not know how, all by itself."

In August, these fields looked like you'd expect to see them in early June. Vicky had always tried to get a second crop of hay and said he was amazed that he had a second this year, and had he had room, there would have been a third. There were several stacks in the creek bottom because the corral was already filled with towering stacks that looked like giant loaves of bread.

Duane was married and had built his house on the south side of the springhouse. He and Vicky had set up a temporary sawmill where they milled all their own wood. A huge saw blade was attached to the differential of a 1954 Chevy pickup. As Vicky put it, "Just a little cowboy know-how goes a long way out here." He showed off their engineering skills of making all the trestles spanning across the roof of the huge attic of Duane's house, and Duane showed me the mounted bear head and claws with the .22 bullet as his trophy of our big hunt, the most vivid of my unforgettable memories.

The End

Printed in the USA
CPSIA information can be obtained
at www.ICGtesting.com
LVHW091227160923
758175LV00002B/605